SPOOK

a ghost comedy

Alan Bowne

BROADWAY PLAY PUBLISHING INC
224 E 62nd St, NY, NY 10065
info@broadwayplaypub.com
www.broadwayplaypub.com

cover photo: Alan Bowne, taken in San Francisco in 1967 when he was 22 years old

I S B N: 978-0-88145-632-5

First printing: November 2015

Book design: Marie Donovan
Page make-up: Adobe Indesign
Typeface: Palatino
Printed and bound in the U S A

PLAYS BY ALAN BOWNE
published by
Broadway Play Publishing Inc

FORTY-DEUCE
first produced in New York in 1981

BEIRUT
first produced in New York in 1987

SHARON AND BILLY
first produced in New York in 1988

CHARACTERS & SETTING

ELEANOR CUMBER, *in her mid-forties, chic, sophisticated, still very attractive, only the lovely lines have grown tense, naked, enamel hard*

LOLLY CUMBER, *her cousin, a couple of years older, simpler, plainer, spritelier*

MR BUTTS, *an Episcopal minister in appropriate garb, about forty years of age, bright and fussy*

THE GHOST, *a strikingly handsome male in his early twenties, 18th Century garb. A non-speaking part*

An old house on the Massachusetts coast. A single set representing a panelled sitting room, rather shabby, of Georgian vintage. French doors giving onto a garden, visible to the audience. Staircase leading to offstage upstairs bedrooms. Entrance door, left. Another door, right, leading to offstage kitchen. Heavy stone fireplace and hearth, over which hangs a large gilt mirror, peeling. The furnishings are of varying quality, the chairs rickety, the tables chipped, the settee and hangings faded. The impression should be one of years of muddled, sporadic attempts to retain the period flavor of the house.

Time: The 1980s.

ACT ONE

Scene 1

(Afternoon. Enter MR BUTTS, *setting down luggage,* ELEANOR CUMBER *following. He bustles beaming into room, while she remains at door. She wears a superbly tailored suit.)*

MR BUTTS: Jeepers! Your cousin has brightened up the place already.

ELEANOR: *(Frigid, looking about doubtfully)* When did she arrive?

MR BUTTS: Didn't I say? A week ago. And *look* at the difference. Well, of course you couldn't know. Your aunt had become such a recluse, poor soul. Come in, Miss Cumber, it's your house now. *(Goes to french doors, calling)* Oh Miss Cumber! *(No response)* Must be down on the rocks. Her car's on the blink, so I volunteered to save you a taxi.

ELEANOR: *(Cold civility; slowly entering)* I'm grateful.

MR BUTTS: I must say it's very brave of you and your cousin.

ELEANOR: Brave?

MR BUTTS: Most people who inherit old houses sell them off at once. To hold onto such a house as this—

ELEANOR: We can always sell it later. After fixing it up. We both decided—

(Trails off, wearily sinking into a chair)

MR BUTTS: Yes, your cousin told me. You both felt the need of a haven. Beautiful word, "haven". One more vowel and it's "heaven".

ELEANOR: I beg your pardon?

MR BUTTS: But to have each decided—I mean, each to have *needed* a haven, living each your different lives *thousands* of miles apart. And to have both been *left* a haven. When you both *needed* it—

ELEANOR: You seem to know a great deal about our needs.

MR BUTTS: Saints alive, I *was* your aunt's executor. I practically *lived* here towards the last. Poor pious lady, she was a great friend to the Church. Funny, her dying that way, down there on the rocks, with her police flash. Apparently she was trying to give conflicting signals to passing ships—it's a treacherous bit of coast along here. No harm done—except she fell and broke her neck. Poor old thing, we assumed she'd gone off her saucer.

ELEANOR: Aunt Cumber was never a well woman.

MR BUTTS: Eccentric. But anyhow your cousin has been dying to see you again.

ELEANOR: And I her.

MR BUTTS: *How* many years?

ELEANOR: Since we've seen each other? We were girls.

MR BUTTS: Amazing. Now tell me about London. It's lovely, isn't it?

ELEANOR: Damp.

MR BUTTS: And Miss Cumber. All those years in California. Must be lovely, California.

ELEANOR: Dry.

MR BUTTS: But then so is Massachusetts lovely. Especially this part. Stretches of coast like this, practically untouched? And this house. Lands sakes, this house is part of our local history.

ELEANOR: Is it?

MR BUTTS: Early Nineteenth Century. I was here so much during your aunt's illness, I fairly made a study of it. Your cousin and I have become great friends on the basis of *that*.

ELEANOR: Have you?

MR BUTTS: Oh yes, but she'll tell you all about it. Where can Miss Cumber be? *(Looks out french doors, then turns back, brightly)* Isn't it fun? When referring to you, we shall be able to say, the Misses Cumber. "How *are* the Misses Cumber?" "Oh, the Misses Cumber are very well, I believe." *So* Nineteenth Century. Like the house.

ELEANOR: Thank you very much.

MR BUTTS: You must be tired. Let me take your bags upstairs.

ELEANOR: Good of you. I am tired.

MR BUTTS: *(Picking up luggage)* Your trunks arrived but two days ago. So many stickers! They certainly *looked* like the trunks of a well-travelled journalist. *(Going up stairs)* International journalists don't often live in this part of Massachusetts, no, I dare say not. We're a bit remote for celebrities, I'm afraid. Oh, we have our smattering of summer people, of course. *(Exits top of stairs)*

(ELEANOR sits, eyes closed. Suddenly she pulls a silver flask from her purse and drinks. Stuffs flask back into purse, shakily dabs lips with handkerchief, as MR BUTTS re-enters, descending stairs)

MR BUTTS: I really do envy you this old house. Our church, now, is a spanking new one. Clean modern lines, acres of glass. Looks like a supermarket, I'm afraid. And I suppose you noticed, the telephone in my *car*? Why, I'm one of God's executives. Will we see *you* at services? Your cousin came last Sabbath—

ELEANOR: *(Exploding; cutting him off)* Yes, I will! *(Beat; composing herself)* Come. If I'm up to it.

MR BUTTS: Well then. I'll just leave you to greet your cousin.

ELEANOR: You've been very helpful.

MR BUTTS: *(Pointing upstairs)* Your room is second door on the left.

ELEANOR: Thank you again.

MR BUTTS: See you soon?

ELEANOR: Good-bye.

(MR BUTTS, pausing by entrance door, clasps hands and looks about.)

MR BUTTS: A wonderful house! *(He exits.)*

(ELEANOR rises, walks about room, distractedly. Bursts into tears and rushes upstairs)

(Beat)

(Enter LOLLY CUMBER from garden, through french doors. She is humming happily, carrying an easel, dressed sloppily in jeans and an old shirt. Brightly she sets down easel, center of room; it holds a watercolor portrait of an extraordinarily handsome young man with hair and clothes in the style of the 18th Century. LOLLY regards it with a frown, laughs, then starts to exit right, into kitchen. Suddenly she pauses, then turns to look up pointedly at top of stairs.)

LOLLY: *(Impishly)* Are you there? *(Beat)* *(Grinning)* You devil! *(Giggling, she exits into kitchen.)*

(Beat)

*(*ELEANOR, *dry-eyed now, descends stairs. Goes to chair, retrieves purse. Takes out flask, starts to drink, then notices painting on easel. Replaces flask and approaches easel. Bemused, she examines it.)*

(Re-enter LOLLY *from kitchen, munching a cookie, unseen by* ELEANOR. LOLLY, *beaming, sneaks up behind her cousin)*

LOLLY: BOO!

*(*ELEANOR *screams.)*

(Blackout)

Scene 2

(The same, over tea. Some moments later. ELEANOR *and* LOLLY, *seated. The easel is now turned to the wall.)*

LOLLY: *(Pouring tea)* This'll fix you up, Eleanor.

ELEANOR: I don't know why I reacted like that.

LOLLY: I'm mortified. It was plain as spit from your letters that you were jumpy, and I should have known better.

ELEANOR: Yes, I even *jumped* on your Mister Butts. He was expecting an "international journalist", not a bundle of nerves.

LOLLY: It was those trunks of yours. Butts is a fiend for romance.

ELEANOR: *Romance?* Writing travel puffs for the British motor trade?

LOLLY: But you've been based in London all these years. That means you *rate*, in this godforsaken backwash. Still, I love our backwash. Always did.

ELEANOR: *(Grimacing; looking about)* Really? Can't say I agree.

LOLLY: And yet—you felt it would do?

ELEANOR: At this point, Lolly, *any* place will do.

LOLLY: (*Sympathetically*) Bad?

ELEANOR: I'll get over it. I have to.

LOLLY: (*Eagerly*) You *are* romantic, Eleanor. Tell me *all* about it.

ELEANOR: What's to tell? I've been thrown over by a married man after ten years of furtive relations.

LOLLY: Well, no one's ever thrown *me* over. Count your blessings.

ELEANOR: Same old Lolly. So what was *your* excuse?

LOLLY: For not marrying? Oh, I had the other kind of thing. The kind where you don't actually *touch* the sonsabitches.

ELEANOR: I see. Unrequited.

LOLLY: Nonexistent's a better word. But anyhow I haven't been destructive or vindictive or insanely jealous and gone about making messes. Haven't had the chance, damn it.

ELEANOR: Wish I could say the same.

LOLLY: Come clean, Eleanor. What was he like?

ELEANOR: So you've been teaching high school all this time?

LOLLY: Art appreciation. Was he tall?

ELEANOR: You must have been a very good teacher.

LOLLY: British right down to his toes?

ELEANOR: Most Englishmen are. You were born to teach, really. You were always so—*organized* as a child.

LOLLY: Yes, I led all the games, didn't I? And if it weren't for those budget cuts, I'd *still* be teaching. (*Gestures, indicating house*) Lucky.

ELEANOR: What is?

LOLLY: This house. And the annuity. Coming as they did, *when* they did. Lucky. *(Warmly)* For both of us.

ELEANOR: Lolly, I want to sleep. Sleep and sleep.

LOLLY: And as for me, I'll trot along the shore, with my easel and watercolors.

ELEANOR: *(Pointing at easel)* Of whom is that portrait?

LOLLY: Oh, nobody. A fantasy.

(Phone rings. LOLLY crosses to it, answers.)

LOLLY: Hello? Hello? *(Looks at phone)* I hate that.

ELEANOR: Heavy breathing?

LOLLY: *(Hanging up)* No. Just silence. Been happening a lot lately.

ELEANOR: Good god. Crank calls in the country. *(Sips tea)* Anyhow, this *tea* is soothing. And Lolly?

LOLLY: *(Sitting)* Hmmmm?

ELEANOR: So are you.

(LOLLY squeezes ELEANOR's hand.)

LOLLY: Yes, even when you were screaming your head off just now, I thought, "Oh, Eleanor hasn't changed a dot." Doesn't seem like twenty-five years. More like twenty-five minutes.

ELEANOR: You were the only cousin I liked. Pity we weren't closer as girls.

LOLLY: Your father detested my mother, my mother thought you were a snot, I *was* a snot, and Aunt Cumber hated the lot of us. Great family for venom.

ELEANOR: When *did* we see each other last?

LOLLY: You graduated Lawrence the year after me, and I went to your commencement. You were—exquisite.

ELEANOR: I was going to Paris. To become a famous writer.

LOLLY: And for me it was New York. To paint "avant-garde" pictures.

ELEANOR: Quaint little phrase.

LOLLY: Isn't it just? Now I prefer the past. After all those years in California—where history began, you know, with the ascension of Dwight David Eisenhower—I've come to treasure it. Even this ugly old house charms me.

ELEANOR: Your Mister Butts tells me he's made a study of it.

LOLLY: He's made a *thing* of it, as they say in Burbank. He's researching all the local records. And I'll be damned if I didn't get sucked into it. Guess what.

ELEANOR: Tell me.

LOLLY: He says Aunt C insisted there was a ghost. I mean maintained it as a fact.

ELEANOR: An ancestral Cumber, no doubt.

LOLLY: Oh, the Cumbers. Mere *arrivistes. They* didn't settle in until after the Civil War. No, there was—someone else here.

ELEANOR: Who?

LOLLY: We aren't certain yet. I just hope he wasn't, you know, commonplace.

ELEANOR: *He?*

LOLLY: Yes, there was a particular man here. There's veiled references to him in the old records. This was a wild stretch of coast in 1812—Tories, sedition, pirates, all that.

ELEANOR: You're hoping for something romantic?

LOLLY: Oh, Butts and I are mad for romance. You don't mind his coming over?

ELEANOR: Oh…no. It's a big house.

LOLLY: I'm even exploring the attic!

ELEANOR: Watch out for bats.

LOLLY: Eleanor. You've been in Europe and places all these years. You forget how little of the past we have in this country. I'm sure Europe just *boils* with history.

ELEANOR: Yes, they're very embarrassed about it.

LOLLY: Damn! Plumb forgot.

ELEANOR: What?

LOLLY: I baked you some scones! To reduce the culture shock.

ELEANOR: *(Distaste)* Scones?

LOLLY: With *heaps* of butter.

ELEANOR: They are a bit dry.

LOLLY: Sit right here. I'll get them.

ELEANOR: Lovely.

(LOLLY *starts for the kitchen; pauses, looks at* ELEANOR)

LOLLY: What was his name?

ELEANOR: Who?

LOLLY: The man. Who threw you over.

ELEANOR: Oh, he had many names. Divine. Exasperating. Cruel. Charming. *(Beat)* Gregory.

LOLLY: You're making my *mouth* water! *(She exits into kitchen)*

(ELEANOR *quickly reaches for her purse. Out of it she pulls the silver flask. Hastily she pours liquor into teacup, replacing flask. Drinks thirstily as:)*

(*Suddenly, behind and unseen by* ELEANOR, THE GHOST *drops into the room by a rope tied around his neck, a cutlass in his teeth. Hangs, shockingly, as if from a gallows. Whips cutlass from teeth and cuts himself down. Teeth bared, his head tilted grotesquely to one side, he approaches* ELEANOR *from behind, his cutlass raised to slash*)

(*Then, from the kitchen, stopping* THE GHOST *in his tracks:*)

LOLLY: These scones looks scrumptious!

(ELEANOR *closes her eyes, fingers to temples.*)

ELEANOR: My god.

(THE GHOST *hastily disappears.*)

(LOLLY *bursts through kitchen door, beaming delightedly. She holds a plate of great, lumpy scones.*)

LOLLY: Tomorrow? I'll make blancmange!

(*Blackout*)

Scene 3

(*The same a few days later.* MR BUTTS *is seated, as* LOLLY, *dressed as before, moves enraptured about the room, fiddling with an ornate lacquered fan and regarding herself in the mirror over the mantle.*)

LOLLY: (*Holding up fan*) It's *gorgeous*!

MR BUTTS: So excited when you phoned. Where did you find it?

LOLLY: In the attic. Under the dust of *centuries* up there, behind *generations* of Cumber stupidity. So go ahead. Explain it.

MR BUTTS: It rang such a bell I couldn't hear myself think!

LOLLY: Out with it, man!

(ELEANOR, *in a flowing silk robe, appears at the top of the stairs*)

MR BUTTS: Well, I've been busy as a ferret, so let me begin at the beginning—

LOLLY: *(Noticing her cousin)* Why, Eleanor.

ELEANOR: Good afternoon, Lolly. Oh, Mister Butts.

MR BUTTS: *(Rising)* Willikers, what a charming robe.

ELEANOR: *(Descending stairs; coldly)* How nice to see you again.

MR BUTTS: And have you settled in these past few days?

ELEANOR: I'm afraid I've been a trifle unwell.

LOLLY: *(Faintly arch; to* MR BUTTS*)* But she's been taking *lots* of liquids.

MR BUTTS: *(To* ELEANOR*)* Poor dear lady. Jet lag?

ELEANOR: I never *lag*, Mister Butts.

(Having descended, ELEANOR *distractedly looks out at garden, fidgets about room, etc, during following.)*

MR BUTTS: *(To* ELEANOR*)* Of course you don't. Aren't you just *delirious* about this old house?

LOLLY: *You* certainly are, Butts. He's been *indefatigable*, Eleanor.

ELEANOR: In what way?

LOLLY: Look at this.

*(*LOLLY *shows fan to* ELEANOR*)*

ELEANOR: *(Examining it briefly)* Where did you get it?

LOLLY: In our attic.

ELEANOR: *(Handing back fan)* Must be rather valuable.

LOLLY: And Butts here can date it for us. It's *pre-*Cumber, of course.

MR BUTTS: I'm convinced it's the same fan.

ELEANOR: The same as what?

LOLLY: He was just about to go into that. Sit down, Eleanor, it's so exciting.

ELEANOR: Oh, don't mind me.

(ELEANOR *continues fidgeting about room as* LOLLY *and* MR BUTTS *sit and converse intently.*)

MR BUTTS: The family that built this house was called Sturdevant. Shipwrights, landowners, and so on. From Nantucket originally. They settled here about 1805, or perhaps a little later—

LOLLY: The hell with the Sturdevants. Get to the good part.

MR BUTTS: Patience, Miss Cumber. Now, this family was hounded out of here into Canada during the second nastiness with England—they were Tories, you see, recusants. But one member of the family remained. A true daughter of the Republic, as it were—

LOLLY: *Hang* the Republic, Butts!

MR BUTTS: Hang *on*, Miss C.

ELEANOR: Lolly?

LOLLY: Yes, sweets?

ELEANOR: You mentioned that Aunt Cumber kept spirits around somewhere? Perhaps Mr. Butts would like a cordial.

MR BUTTS: How *very* kind.

LOLLY: *(Eyebrow raised in a knowing way)* Sure. There, in the sideboard. There's cordial. Port. Glasses in the cabinet.

ELEANOR: *(Crossing to sideboard)* And you, Lolly?

LOLLY: Too early for me, thanks. Plow on, Butts!

(ELEANOR *prepares drinks—cordial for* MR BUTTS, *a brimming glass of port for herself—during the fallowing.*)

MR BUTTS: Well. This sole remaining Sturdevant got the family's abandoned fortune, of course. A patriotic lady, quiet, churchgoing—naturally everyone *was*, in those days—

LOLLY: *(Impatiently)* It was a simpler world, Butts, no doubt about it.

MR BUTTS: And then suddenly, when she was a perfectly *respectable* old maid of forty-five—

(Abruptly MR BUTTS *pauses, embarrassed.* LOLLY *and* ELEANOR *appraise him ironically.)*

MR BUTTS: Well, I mean, of course, that forty-five was old for *those* days—

ELEANOR: *(Handing him cordial)* Here's your *foot*, Mr. Butts.

LOLLY: Onward, onward.

MR BUTTS: *(Taking drink)* Dear lady, thank you. So the woman suddenly, at the, for then, advanced age of forty-five, during the aftermath of our second dispute with Mother England, took to her bosom, believe it or not, a rosy youth of twenty-two!

LOLLY: *(Outraged)* No!

*(*ELEANOR, *having returned to sideboard, downs her glass of port in one gulp)*

MR BUTTS: Not unusual for today, these May-December things, not at all. But in those days, you understand, it raised quite a scandal.

LOLLY: *(Rising)* Don't you *dare* tell me that he was a— *gigolo!*

ELEANOR: *(Pouring another)* He?

LOLLY: The man we've been researching. Our—
rumored ghost.

ELEANOR: *(Downing her second drink)* Good lord, Lolly.

LOLLY: I won't have a *smarmy* sort of ghost around
here. No way.

ELEANOR: Heaven forfend.

MR BUTTS: He wasn't like that, I think. No, that's not
my impression at all. A dashing sort, is my image.
A very handsome and venturesome youth, by all
accounts.

LOLLY: *(Sitting again)* Venturesome, all right. Preying
on wealthy women in their prime.

MR BUTTS: He was a soldier and a sailor, had picked
up manners and an education—all this by the age
of twenty-two. He was considered a "catch" by the
neighborhood. And of course Miss Sturdevant was *mad*
for him. She even, brazenly, attended his trial—

LOLLY: Trial?

MR BUTTS: *Dear* Miss Cumber. Here's the good part. He
was a— *(Triumphant beat) Smuggler!*

LOLLY: *(Rising, to herself mostly)* I knew it! He *wasn't*
vulgar! He *can't* have been!

(ELEANOR regards LOLLY with interest.)

MR BUTTS: You'd think, with her fortune and his
prospects, that he'd have given it up. But he seems to
have had a passion for it—

LOLLY: Of course he did. He was a passionate creature.

ELEANOR: Lolly, what are you talking about?

LOLLY: Our *ghost*, Eleanor.

MR BUTTS: *(To ELEANOR)* Yes, your aunt was *convinced*
there was a ghost here. A young, *male* ghost.

ELEANOR: Aunt Cumber was a knucklehead.

MR BUTTS: Eccentric.

LOLLY: Who's denying *that*? But just imagine, Eleanor.
(Fanning herself) I'm carried away by the *idea* of a ghost.
As they say in Burbank, I'm *behind* the idea. *(Clasps fan,
looks at it. To* MR BUTTS:*)* But what about this?

MR BUTTS: Oh, that's the detail that made it all click.
His trial for smuggling was a local event. They caught
him, middle of the night, at Drubbers Cove, a few
miles north. Liquor. Firearms. The others got away,
him they caught—

LOLLY: But of course he *disdained* his captors. He was
too proud to resist.

MR BUTTS: Proud, very proud. At his trial he stood in
the dock and never said a word. And she, his recent
bride, that respectable Sturdevant heiress, brazenly—
or to my mind courageously—sat there, through the
whole trial, her eyes never moving from his face—

LOLLY: She loved him. Passionately.

MR BUTTS: Oh yes, passionately! And through it all, as
it was repeatedly remarked, she held to her breast an
ornate lacquered fan, a wedding gift from her young
husband. They hadn't been married a week.

*(*LOLLY *stares at fan.)*

LOLLY: Bingo! Then this must be—*booty*!

MR BUTTS: No doubt. He was very active in that line, as
it turned out. Evidence poured in that he was involved
in capers all up and down—

LOLLY: *My god! (She drops fan, as if it were on fire)*

MR BUTTS: Miss C! What's the matter?

LOLLY: It's red hot!

ELEANOR: Lolly, don't be absurd!

LOLLY: But, Eleanor

ELEANOR: *(Secreting port decanter under robe)* I need to rest. If you'll both excuse me. All this *excitement*—

LOLLY: Eleanor, it was *burning*!

ELEANOR: Enjoy yourselves. Good afternoon, Mister Butts.

MR BUTTS: *(Rising)* Dear Miss Cumber.

(ELEANOR ascends staircase and exits, MR BUTTS looking after her. LOLLY has gingerly picked up fan; studies it.)

MR BUTTS: Poor lady. She's not happy here?

LOLLY: *(Glancing at sideboard)* Oh, she has her comforts. *(Slowly working fan again)* So what happened?

MR BUTTS: *(Referring to fan)* I don't know. Is it still hot?

LOLLY: Oh, it must have been my imagination. I meant, what happened to *him*? Our ghost.

MR BUTTS: *(Seating himself)* Well, what *could* happen? Capital offense. They hanged him.

LOLLY: Of course! They hanged him. I mean, it had to be *something* like that.

MR BUTTS: Yes, and she watched that, too. Never took her eyes from his face.

LOLLY: How in hell could you?

MR BUTTS: Pardon me?

LOLLY: Well, you said he was handsome. And what happened to *her*?

MR BUTTS: She went mad, the poor impassioned thing. Died raving. The fortune reverted to distant relations and the house remained, then, vacant for some years. Then your ancestors bought it.

LOLLY: And with that, the story ends!

MR BUTTS: Oh, on the contrary. You've some very respectable forebears—

LOLLY: *(Raising her hand)* Spare me the Cumbers! *(Sitting)* Well, now, that *is* fascinating. Well done, Butts. More cordial?

MR BUTTS: *(Checking watch)* Jeepers, I must get going. Even ministers have duties. But don't think I've completed my research on your wonderful house.

LOLLY: *(Looking at fan)* But we know the essentials now, don't we? Except—what was his name?

MR BUTTS: Our smuggler? It's variously spelled. Something like Smithers.

LOLLY: It can't have been *Smithers*!

MR BUTTS: Plain Smythe, perhaps.

LOLLY: Impossible. I'm sure his name was assumed anyhow. Probably his real name was something like— Gregory.

MR BUTTS: Gregory?

LOLLY: Aunt C didn't much like him, did she?

MR BUTTS: The apparition? Oh no, she was quite crusty about him. Especially when he'd appear at the top of the stairs, or out those french doors. Called the police, once.

LOLLY: The old bitch!

MR BUTTS: Dear me.

LOLLY: Sorry, Butts. But if *I* were to see a ghost, I should be pleased about it. It's a distinction, in a way, isn't it?

MR BUTTS: All the great houses in England have resident ghosts.

LOLLY: Exactly.

MR BUTTS: *(Rising)* Well, I shall continue my research, you can be sure of that.

LOLLY: *(Also rising)* Search on, search on, old Butts. Find out all you can about this fellow.

(LOLLY accompanies MR BUTTS to door.)

MR BUTTS: Indeed I shall. You know, your coming here has meant a great deal to me.

LOLLY: How so?

MR BUTTS: Well, most people here are indifferent to local history. Your interest has been—willikers, I suppose I've been a bit lonely in my passion for the past.

LOLLY: *(Pumping his hand)* You can count on me, Butts. I'm *interested*!

(Suddenly, a shattering scream from upstairs. A dishevelled ELEANOR comes rushing down the staircase)

ELEANOR: *Mister Butts!* You're not leaving, are you? Good lord, we've hardly talked at all. Have another cordial!

MR BUTTS: Dear lady, I—

(LOLLY stares intently at ELEANOR.)

ELEANOR: *(Rapidfire)* Now, now, I won't hear of your leaving. After all, I'm new to the neighborhood. Who *are* our neighbors anyhow? Nice people? *(Seating herself on settee, patting cushion next to her)* Come right over here and tell me all about them. The house should be filled with talk, yes, lots and lots of animated talk—

MR BUTTS: Oh, do let me take a rain check, Miss Cumber—

ELEANOR: Lolly, make him stay. I'm feeling better now, and in the mood for people, people, shall we throw a housewarming?

LOLLY: Butts is leaving. *(Staring at* ELEANOR, *she hands hat to* MR BUTTS*)* Good-bye, Butts.

MR BUTTS: Oh yes, I really must go. *(To* ELEANOR*)* But Miss Cumber, I shall be delighted at some point—

LOLLY: Good-*bye*, Butts.

MR BUTTS: *(Bowing)* Ladies.

*(*LOLLY *shows* MR BUTTS *out. She moves slowly back into room, as* ELEANOR *crosses nervously to sideboard)*

LOLLY: What's the matter, Eleanor?

ELEANOR: I could use a cordial myself.

LOLLY: Why not port? Of course you took the decanter up to your room.

*(*ELEANOR, *trembling at sideboard, spills cordial)*

ELEANOR: *Hell!*

LOLLY: Fess up, Eleanor!

ELEANOR: *(Hands to her face)* All *right!* I *drink!*

(The phone rings. ELEANOR *grabs it)*

ELEANOR: Hello? *Hello? (Beat)* Who is it? *(Looks at receiver)* I'm going mad.

LOLLY: Forget the crank call, Eleanor. *(Triumphantly:)* You've seen him!

(Blackout)

Scene 4

(The same, next morning. A drizzle perceptible in the garden. LOLLY, *sloppily dressed as before, is at her easel. She dabs, scowls, rips away paper and starts again.* ELEANOR *appears at head of stairs, in tight blouse and slacks, looking silken, curvaceous.)*

LOLLY: Why, Eleanor. Up early. Lousy rain. Pretty blouse.

ELEANOR: (*Descending*) I felt like dressing. I've been slovenly long enough.

LOLLY: Slovenly? You make *me* feel dowdy. But then you always did, damn it.

ELEANOR: You've a charm of your own, Lolly. What other woman could bring off blue jeans at your age?

LOLLY: Hot coffee in the kitchen.

ELEANOR: (*Crossing*) Marvellous.

LOLLY: (*Casually*) Did you see him again?

ELEANOR: No, but I *felt* him, his presence, the whole night. Rather a tease, isn't he?

LOLLY: Not with me.

(*Beat, as* ELEANOR *pauses on her way to kitchen*)

ELEANOR: I beg your pardon?

LOLLY: There's oatmeal on the stove.

ELEANOR: Thank you. (*She exits into kitchen.*)

LOLLY: (*Calling to* ELEANOR) So. He's taken to haunting *your* room for a change. Orange juice in the fridge.

ELEANOR: (*Off*) Just coffee, thanks. And a bit of this toast. (*Re-enters with a cup of coffee and a slice of toast in the saucer*) I'd hardly call it "haunting". He's very *fine*, isn't he?

LOLLY: He's got what Californians call an "aura".

ELEANOR: (*Seating herself*) Like the feel of old Spanish lace.

LOLLY: Oh my. They wouldn't make an observation like that In Burbank.

ELEANOR: Tell me, has your Mister Butts seen the ghost?

LOLLY: Oh no, he's excited by the pure romance of it. He'd have a cat if he actually saw him. Butts is basically a sweet, timid, researching old—

ELEANOR: *Ponce.*

LOLLY: Eleanor!

ELEANOR: And our ghost wasn't with *you* at all last night?

LOLLY: *(Busily painting)* No.

ELEANOR: Well, of course I'm new.

LOLLY: Right. It's natural he'd be curious.

ELEANOR: I don't mean to monopolize him.

LOLLY: Never fear. He's *quite* gregarious.

(Beat, as ELEANOR *watches* LOLLY *paint)*

ELEANOR: You're so *comfy* about him, Lolly. I can't believe you were here alone with him for an entire week. When *I* actually saw him yesterday, there by my bed, I thought—well, I thought I'd gone nuts.

LOLLY: Understandable, sweets. You'd been drinking buckets of port.

ELEANOR: *(Laughing)* Yes, after I'd run through all the scotch in my trunk. He was…sobering. Weren't *you* frightened, at first?

LOLLY: What, did you think he was a burglar or something?

ELEANOR: You're right. Hardly looks like a second-storey man, does he? More like a too-handsome actor out of a Hollywood costume epic. *Anthony Adverse.* No, not a thug, but definitely—*queer.*

LOLLY: He's like no fellow alive today. You can tell that at a glance.

ELEANOR: Especially the funny way he holds his head.

LOLLY: Oh, there's nothing *funny* about it. Butts explained that. *(Pointing with brush at fireplace)*

You know, we could conserve on heat by burning wood in there.

ELEANOR: Oh, I love a fire. What did he say?

LOLLY: I'll order in a chord. Butts? He'll yak your ear off. Weren't you listening yesterday?

ELEANOR: I was in and out of the room, remember?

LOLLY: Oh right. Smuggling the decanter upstairs.

ELEANOR: Why haven't you told Mister Butts that you've actually encountered the ghost?

LOLLY: I don't know. A scruple, I guess. If the ghost wanted to meet Butts, then he'd show himself to the man.

ELEANOR: As he did to me.

LOLLY: A glimpse, yes. He did give you a tiny glimpse.

ELEANOR: I also *felt* him, Lolly. His presence. All night.

LOLLY: Oh, I always see him *and* feel him.

ELEANOR: Until last night, darling.

LOLLY: Obviously he's *shyer* where you're concerned.

ELEANOR: Or subtler.

LOLLY: Oh, he's very subtle. The eyes.

ELEANOR: Grotesque, all the same.

LOLLY: I feel privileged.

ELEANOR: Oh, I don't mean it's grotesque having a ghost. I mean his twisted neck.

LOLLY: I think it's a distinction.

ELEANOR: Having a ghost? Darling, of course it is.

LOLLY: I meant the way he holds his head. It's distinct. And distinguished.

ELEANOR: But *why* is his neck twisted?

LOLLY: It's a minor point in his appearance. *(Beat)* He was hung, of course.

ELEANOR: Hung?

LOLLY: By the neck. Until dead. Like this morning, for instance. I hardly noticed it.

ELEANOR: *(Quickly)* You saw him this morning?

LOLLY: Of course.

ELEANOR: Are you sure? *I* haven't seen him.

LOLLY: Oh, he shows himself to *me* with a kind of—I don't know, a kind of abandon.

(Beat, as ELEANOR *watches* LOLLY *paint)*

ELEANOR: Hung, did you say? How delightful. Mister Butts said he was a—*criminal*, or something?

LOLLY: Not a criminal. An adventurer. Quite a tale. Get the story from Butts.

ELEANOR: Who, I'm sure, is fascinated by our ghost's tale. *(As if to herself)* No, he wouldn't show himself to a creature like Mister Butts. Or *would* he?

LOLLY: He hardly showed himself to you.

ELEANOR: Yes, I *think* our ghost prefers women. But you can't always tell with that sort, can you?

(Beat, as LOLLY *pauses in her daubing. Looking at* ELEANOR:*)*

LOLLY: What are you saying?

ELEANOR: Well, there's a certain *delicacy* in his appearance—but it's more in the feeling you get, actually. Something feline, almost feminine.

LOLLY: *(Shocked)* Do you doubt his—his *tendencies*?

ELEANOR: No, I suppose not.

LOLLY: What a *nasty* little suspicion—

ELEANOR: He's a bit *smooth*, though, isn't he?

LOLLY: He's elegant, that's all—it was the period. You've only seen him that once.

ELEANOR: But I *felt* him, Lolly. Brushing against me. All night.

LOLLY: There's probably a *draft* in your room.

ELEANOR: Well, after all, he wasn't with *you*, was he?

(Beat, as LOLLY *angrily returns to painting.* ELEANOR, *agitated, looks away.* LOLLY *glances at her cousin, sidelong, and, casually as possible, says:)*

LOLLY: So he—actually *brushed* against you?

ELEANOR: Yes, all night. *(Shivering)* A light stirring of the hairs on my arms.

LOLLY: Oh, is *that* all?

ELEANOR: What do you mean?

LOLLY: *(Laying down brush; casually)* Do you want your oatmeal?

ELEANOR: *What* do you mean, Lolly?

LOLLY: Eleanor, I can't help it if he's more *demonstrative* where I'm concerned, can I? *(Picks up* ELEANOR's *cup)* More coffee?

(Beat, as ELEANOR *regards her cousin)*

ELEANOR: Yes, thank you.

LOLLY: *(Rising)* I'll get it for you.

ELEANOR: Darling, you're always waiting on me.

LOLLY: Oh, I enjoy it.

ELEANOR: Yes, I know.

LOLLY: *(Crossing to kitchen)* Know what?

ELEANOR: About that motherly streak in you.

(LOLLY *halts at kitchen door*)

LOLLY: That's pretty funny, corning from someone my own age.

ELEANOR: I'm not exactly your age, Lolly.

LOLLY: Eleanor, there's not two years between us.

ELEANOR: Oh, I don't mean to disparage. Some men adore motherly types.

LOLLY: I'll be damned if I'm a motherly type!

ELEANOR: Darling, it's one of the many nicest things about you.

LOLLY: *(Replaces cup; returns to easel)* It's on the stove. Bowls in the cupboard.

ELEANOR: Now I've made you angry.

LOLLY: *(Furiously painting)* Life hasn't been kind to you, has it, Eleanor?

ELEANOR: Meaning?

LOLLY: You've hardened. It's no wonder he was so— *fleeting.*

ELEANOR: I see. *(Beat)* Is that the portrait you were working on when I arrived? Of our young ghost?

LOLLY: It's a seascape.

ELEANOR: Darling, what shall we do about this—*spook*?

LOLLY: *(Bridling at word)* Simply remain very still. And very proud.

ELEANOR: He can't exactly be a *benign* spirit, can he?

LOLLY: You don't know him, Eleanor.

ELEANOR: He died violently.

LOLLY: Aunt C lived here quite comfortably for many years.

ELEANOR: Did he spend entire nights in *her* room? *Pussyfooting* around?

LOLLY: He doesn't—*pussyfoot!*

ELEANOR: You know, they're finding out that most of those pirates were rather more *swish* than swash

(LOLLY *slams down her brush.*)

LOLLY: Eleanor! You scarcely even *saw* him!

ELEANOR: Lolly Cumber! You're in love with him!

LOLLY: I am not!

ELEANOR: I can't believe it!

LOLLY: I *admire* him!

ELEANOR: *Lovelorn?* For a *spectre*???

LOLLY: Well, at least I'm not *devious* about it! *(Quick change:)* More coffee?

ELEANOR: *(Quick change also; hands her the cup)* That would be nice. Devious?

LOLLY: *(Crossing to kitchen)* I'm not trying to hide *my* real feelings. Am I?

(*Beat, as* LOLLY *exits into kitchen.*)

(ELEANOR *rises, thoughtful, and crosses to easel. Regards watercolor critically, takes brush and touches it up as:*)

LOLLY: *(Calling from kitchen, off)* Cream and sugar?

ELEANOR: Please.

LOLLY: Oatmeal?

ELEANOR: Lovely.

LOLLY: Cream and sugar on that, too?

ELEANOR: Gobs and heaps.

LOLLY: Yummy.

ELEANOR: Quite.

(ELEANOR *sits again as* LOLLY *re-enters with tray holding cup of coffee and bowl of oatmeal*)

LOLLY: *(Setting down tray)* I feel so *English* here. Close your eyes, Eleanor. We could be on the Cornish coast.

ELEANOR: The Cornish coast is dreary. What did you mean, when you said he was more *demonstrative* with you?

LOLLY: What do you care? Not two minutes ago you were writing him off as a soft, *faggy* sort of ghost. How's the oatmeal? Is it nice?

ELEANOR: *(Tasting it)* Fine, thanks. Answer the question.

LOLLY: *(Regarding watercolor)* I put too much red there.

ELEANOR: Take it from me, these are deep waters, Lolly. You're older in years, but—

LOLLY: *(Retouching watercolor)* Two years older and *what* are you going on about?

ELEANOR: I'm talking about romantic notions. A naive woman like you—

LOLLY: He's a ghost!

ELEANOR: He can still hurt you.

LOLLY: A ghost, Eleanor. A phenomenon, a visitation, an extrasensory bonanza!

ELEANOR: With no more than a glance, across a room. Or flitting by in an airport. With nothing more than his eyes, a man can peel the skin, painfully, in strips, right off your body.

LOLLY: Who's romantic now, Eleanor?

ELEANOR: You musn't get emotionally involved, Lolly.

LOLLY: *(Furiously painting)* How can one *not*? He *lives* here!

ELEANOR: Men are manipulative swine, Lolly. Rooting among us with their piggy little snouts—

LOLLY: *(Throwing down brush)* This is as different from one of *your* affairs as—as—as porridge is from good red pudding!

ELEANOR: You're incoherent!

LOLLY: And you're paranoid!

ELEANOR: *(Mimics her cousin)* "More demonstrative with me!" *(Slams down bowl)* What in *hell* did you mean by that?

LOLLY: But I am *not* paranoid! I do *not* go about making up deceitful—*theories*:

ELEANOR: Deceitful *what*?

LOLLY: Theories, about his *obvious* masculinity. Repressed, dirty little theories. To hide an *attraction* to him. Hell, I *acknowledge* his masculinity. I admire and quietly *honor* it! As part of his beautiful spell.

(Beat)

ELEANOR: How far have you gone with this—spook?

LOLLY: *(Rising)* Stop calling him that!

ELEANOR: How far, Lolly? I'm telling you. There's something about him. Something not right. He *wants* something.

LOLLY: Ridiculous. What could a *ghost* require?

ELEANOR: *This* ghost? There's no telling.

LOLLY: You don't *know* him! *(She snatches up an antique laquered fan from a table and crosses at once to french doors. She opens them, breathes deeply. She stands there looking out into the rain, trembling, working the fan—it flutters like a crazed moth.)* He's a pure and—splendid spirit.

ELEANOR: You're very far gone. I had no idea.

LOLLY: Be quiet, Eleanor.

(Beat. ELEANOR *digs into her oatmeal. Between mouthfuls, and punctuated by* LOLLY's *stop-and-go fanwork:)*

ELEANOR: Sticks to your ribs, this stuff. I had a friend. In London. Lovely girl. No longer young, but pretty, outgoing. Apparently self-destructive. Unfortunate. All her affairs? Disasters. Worse sort of luck with men. My, this oatmeal is creamy. Finally she fell in love with a bloke rather younger than herself—charm? You wouldn't have believed the tart, pineapply impression he made when he smiled. Took her money, of course. Trips to Majorca. Even his toothpaste had a designer label. Made her lease a flat, dreadfully dear, for them to live in. And as soon as she'd put down the money? He was gone. Ta-ta. Sorry. Won't work. But that wasn't the worst. *(Puts down the bowl with a grimace)* A little of this goes a long way. He took up with someone else directly after her, a married chiropractor in Chalk Farm. A man, of course. Older, of course. Wealthy, to be sure. I mean, you never can tell about the *pretty* ones. They always want *everything*, Lolly, the last drop—even, I shouldn't wonder, beyond the grave. There's a pure, destructive force in some men, darling, and I suspect it never dies.

LOLLY: *I won't! Let you spoil it!* (She exits, rushing into the rainy garden.)

(Beat, as ELEANOR *quietly sips her coffee. Suddenly, She freezes. Looks over her shoulder. Shivers:)*

ELEANOR: You're here, aren't you? *(Rises, cup in hand, looking about)* Why don't you show yourself? My, such a *wimpy* little ghost. *(A high, giggling sound)* All right, don't. Obviously you prefer that silly, *sketching* little person. Oh, I understand. She's not like me, is she? Oh no. With me you'd have to can the romance, boyo. And *put out!* (The sound of numerous smacking kisses)

Oh, aren't we coy? Stick with Lolly, by all means. Or why not show yourself to Mister Butts? Fluff haunting fluff—it's perfect. Since you're evidently incapable of being—*demonstrative* with me.

(Suddenly the cup jerks in ELEANOR'*s hand, its contents splashing directly into her face.)*

ELEANOR:*(Dropping cup, wiping face)* Oh, cute. Very cute. Surely the big bad ghost can do better than that. *(Suddenly, she staggers backwards, as if fending off an attacker, wildly clawing the air.)*

*(*ELEANOR'*s clothes break away, revealing lacy underthings, and she screams.)*

(Abruptly she lands with thud on the floor. Silence)

(She scrambles to her hands and knees, glaring about her.)

ELEANOR: No rough stuff, honey! *Understand? (Silence. She rises to her feet, trying to cover herself)* Honey? *(Silence. She looks wildly about room.)* Honey?

(Blackout)

END OF ACT ONE

ACT TWO

Scene 5

(A week later, morning. Sunlight from the garden. LOLLY *descends stairs, sporting ribbons in her newly coiffed hair, wearing a crisp high-necked robe trimmed in lace. She is toying with the antique lacquered fan. She crosses to mantle and poses against it, hautily; then She sits demurely in a chair, eyebrows arched, working the fan; then SHE drapes herself regally over the settee—each time making a picture, as if for an imaginary spectator.* ELEANOR, *drastically changed in baggy jeans, down-at-heels loafers, and shapeless blouse, appears at top of stairs, watching* LOLLY, *unseen by her. Finally, belligerently:)*

ELEANOR: What in blazes are you doing?

LOLLY: *(Startled)* What? Oh, Eleanor. Up so early?

ELEANOR: *(Descending)* Why so surprised? I've been cracking the dawn for a week.

LOLLY: Fess up, Eleanor. What about my new robe? Drove into town specially to get it.

ELEANOR: *(Sarcastic)* Me, I'm for the seashells. I'm just crazy for seashells. Want to come?

LOLLY: No, thank you. Be careful of the rocks. Butts is popping by.

ELEANOR: A daily occurrence of late. Is there coffee?

LOLLY: No, would you be a dear and make some?

ELEANOR: No scones? No oatmeal? *No pop tarts???*

LOLLY: I think you need coffee, Eleanor.

ELEANOR: Do you? *(Crosses to sideboard, takes out bottle and pours a drink) This* will get me started.

LOLLY: Been up all night?

ELEANOR: *(Drinking)* Kept hearing strange sounds.

LOLLY: You've become so damned outdoorsy. But I worry about you down on those rocks.

ELEANOR: Well, not strange so much as—*vigorous.*

LOLLY: You're in no shape for messing round those rocks, sweets.

ELEANOR: *(Pouring another) You* couldn't have got much sleep either.

LOLLY: Me? I sleep like the dead.

ELEANOR: *(Slamming down bottle)* Apparently you sleep *with* the dead!

LOLLY: Cut out the sauce, Eleanor.

ELEANOR: You don't approve of my drinking?

LOLLY: No. Should I?

ELEANOR: But everyone has a special vice.

LOLLY: Yours is dangerous.

ELEANOR: So is yours.

LOLLY: *(Rising; breezily)* Here I've been such a frump all this time, and now I've this new permanent and you haven't even mentioned it.

ELEANOR: You used to be such a busy, frantically *butch* little woman, and now—

LOLLY: *(Twirling)* And now feast your eyes!

(ELEANOR crosses to mantle and lights cigarette from box)

ELEANOR: You could have borrowed something of mine. After all, *I've* no one to impress but the seagulls.

LOLLY: I've snapped in a new cassette, as they say in Burbank. I'm entering a new phase. It's this fan. I've got a *thing* for it. You can't go around in jeans and bring off a fan like this.

ELEANOR: It doesn't *burn* you anymore?

LOLLY: Oh, let it burn!

ELEANOR: *Why don't I see him, Lolly?*

LOLLY: Those jeans I loaned you, Eleanor, don't they seem a bit *floppy*—?

ELEANOR: He isn't—*real*! We've been imagining him!

LOLLY: Who? Our *poncey* old ghost?

ELEANOR: You're making up those sounds in the night! To rattle me!

LOLLY: Am I? Sorry.

ELEANOR: You can't even do it *accurately*!

LOLLY: How *dare* you!

(A knocking at entrance door. Quick change:)

ELEANOR: And here's your Mister Butts. *(Grabbing up a basket and stashing bottle into it)* My cue to make for the beach.

LOLLY: *(Cold)* Watch yourself on those rocks, Eleanor.

ELEANOR: Look out for yourself, Lolly. *(She exits through french doors.)*

(LOLLY admits MR BUTTS.)

MR BUTTS: Jeepers! You look wonderful, Miss C.

LOLLY: *(Grandly)* Don't stop.

MR BUTTS: Elegant. Regal.

LOLLY: I *feel* like royalty. Haven't done a thing all morning but admire myself. I'll make some coffee.

MR BUTTS: Dear lady, I can't stay. Just came by to share a little more of my research, then I have to be off. Fundraising affair for the church.

LOLLY: How very dull. Sit down, Butts.

MR BUTTS: Thank you.

(LOLLY *and* MR BUTTS *sit.*)

MR BUTTS: And how is Miss Cumber?

LOLLY: Drunk as a skunk. But desperately active. Tottering tipsily all over the rocks down there.

MR BUTTS: Willikers. That's dangerous.

LOLLY: Babies and drunks, you know.

MR BUTTS: They've a special providence, yes.

LOLLY: Listen, Butts. I've definitely decided to call him Gregory. It's more in tune. So that's how we'll refer to him from now on.

MR BUTTS: Oh, but I *like* Smithers.

LOLLY: It's common. We're canning it.

MR BUTTS: Strange, how almost three-dimensional he's become for us.

LOLLY: Yes. But we get at his essence, you see, with Gregory.

MR BUTTS: Well, I'm here to tell you, his essence had a lingering effect.

LOLLY: We know *that*. Haven't we accepted the idea that there is, *must* be, a ghost here somewhere? And isn't that idea our bond?

MR BUTTS: Of course—it's our harmless but beautiful conceit. I meant on poor Miss Sturdevant.

LOLLY: Gregory's wife?

(Unseen by either LOLLY *or* MR BUTTS, THE GHOST *appears in garden, through french doors, stripped to the waist. He yawns, shaking his lopsided head blearily. Turns away from audience and, during following, pisses into a flower bed)*

MR BUTTS: The very same. The lady of the fan. Our spirited young Spirit. That poor, impassioned forty-five year-old.

LOLLY: Yes, yes, well what of her?

MR BUTTS: I believe I told you she went mad? Well, I've unearthed an old medical report that tells us why.

LOLLY: No doubt it was grief.

MR BUTTS: No. Guilt.

LOLLY: Guilt?

MR BUTTS: The story the poor lady told, before going completely mad, was this. Her dead husband had *spoken* to her, can you imagine? From beyond the grave. Wanting her to do something—she wouldn't specify what, but something that violated her conscience. The tension, and the guilt, drove her insane.

LOLLY: *Do* something?

MR BUTTS: Something bad, apparently.

LOLLY: *Bad?* Impossible. *(Slaps* MR BUTTS's *wrist with fan) Our* ghost?

MR BUTTS: You're right. Inconceivable.

(After relieving himself, THE GHOST *passes into room and listens, still unseen.)*

LOLLY: *(Expansive)* He wanted her to do something—something—

MR BUTTS: What *could* it have been?

LOLLY: Anyhow, she faltered? She wouldn't do it?

MR BUTTS: I'm afraid so.

LOLLY: I always suspected it.

MR BUTTS: What?

LOLLY: That she loved him, but not enough.

MR BUTTS: Whatever it was he asked, it went against her grain.

LOLLY: But they were all such *puritans* then. I'm sure it wasn't bad in the large, the liberal, the encompassing view. He *isn't* petty. Not our Gregory.

MR BUTTS: He was above the local mores, certainly.

LOLLY: As I say, the poor woman simply faltered.

MR BUTTS: Tragic.

LOLLY: Sad.

MR BUTTS: Well, in any case,I thought you'd like to know.

LOLLY: It doesn't change anything.

MR BUTTS: Oh no.

LOLLY: We're still *behind* the ghost.

MR BUTTS: All the way.

LOLLY: She didn't understand. She was trapped by her upbringing, by her time and place.

MR BUTTS: That's it. Exactly. *My* image of him isn't tarnished.

LOLLY: Rather enhanced. After all, what *could* he have asked but that she be—*heroic*?

(Hand over mouth, as if snickering, THE GHOST, *still unseen by the room's inhabitants, turns and disappears)*

MR BUTTS: *(Sitting edge of chair; eagerly)* Oh yes! That was my deep thought, but I couldn't utter it. I wanted to be sure you had it too, that your faith in him was *unshakeable*!

LOLLY: What *could* it have been, but that she live in a large, daring way?

MR BUTTS: That she rise to *his* standard.

LOLLY: Best way to honor *his* memory!

(ELEANOR *at once appears at french doors, unseen by others.*)

MR BUTTS: He wanted her, perhaps, to break away and see the world! As *he* had seen it! Europe, Polynesia

LOLLY: Keep the faith, Butts!

MR BUTTS: How *gorgeous* he must have been!

(*Enter* ELEANOR *from garden, swinging basket*)

ELEANOR: Mister Butts! You act as if that seat is wet.

LOLLY: (*Startled*) Damn it, Eleanor! You scared the bejesus out of me.

ELEANOR: I got bored down on the rocks.

MR BUTTS: Dear lady, what a surprise. Shell collecting?

ELEANOR: Yes indeedy. Want to see? Look at this cylindrical one.

MR BUTTS: (*Examining shell*) Very nice.

LOLLY: Butts was just leaving.

ELEANOR: (*To* MR BUTTS) Nice? It's gross. See how long and stiff it is, how round, firm, tumescent—?

MR BUTTS: (*Nervously*) I've got to go.

LOLLY: Thanks for dropping by, Butts.

ELEANOR: But you're *always* excluding me from your little tit-a-tits. Spirits, that's what we need.

(ELEANOR *crosses to sideboard to fix a drink*)

MR BUTTS: (*Rising*) Oh, Miss Cumber, too early for me.

(LOLLY *rises and hustles* MR BUTTS *towards the door.*)

LOLLY: *(To* MR BUTTS, *under her breath)* She'll never understand us. *(Normal tones)*

Good-bye, Butts.

ELEANOR: *(Spinning round)* Why are you *whispering*? You act like a couple of *poofters* hissing about my *panty line*!

LOLLY: Good god, Eleanor, take a nap!

ELEANOR: But what's the conspiracy?

LOLLY: What do you care? You treat us like fools.

ELEANOR: Touchy!

LOLLY: And the contempt you show this poor man is unforgiveable.

MR BUTTS: Oh no, dear lady, please—

ELEANOR: Where is he, Lolly?

LOLLY: Who?

ELEANOR: The *third party* to all this giggling and whispering. The man I saw. When I was down on the rocks. Entering through the garden.

LOLLY: *(To* MR BUTTS) She's drunk.

ELEANOR: Cozy, aren't we? Secretive. Out-shutting.

MR BUTTS: *(To* ELEANOR) Dear Miss Cumber, your cousin and I simply share some harmless little conceits about the past—

ELEANOR: *(Turning on* MR BUTTS) And you! You're as excited as a schoolgirl!

LOLLY: That's enough, Eleanor. Your innuendoes are disgusting.

ELEANOR: Are they?

LOLLY: But not surprising, coming from a woman who chased after a *pervert* for ten years!

(Beat)

ELEANOR: *(Stunned)* What—are you—saying?

LOLLY: Forgive her, Butts. She endured a terrible experience in England. Mad for a man who wasn't—normal.

MR BUTTS: You mean—?

LOLLY: Exactly. He dished her for a male chiropractor.

MR BUTTS: A chiropractor? *(To* ELEANOR*)* How awful for you.

ELEANOR: *(Staring at* LOLLY*)* What a filthy, filthy, filthy lie.

LOLLY: *(To* ELEANOR*)* I wasn't fooled by that story you told. You weren't talking about a *friend*. You were telling our own story. That's why I was so upset. I *pitied* you.

ELEANOR: *(Hysterical laugh)* Gregory? A—*homo*?

MR BUTTS: Gregory?

LOLLY: *(To* MR BUTTS*)* Took her money. Wrecked her life. As a result? Paranoid.

ELEANOR: Leave it to a romantic, raddled old *virgin* to invent such a—such a— *(Bursting into tears, she rushes for the stairs)*

MR BUTTS: *(Reaching out to* ELEANOR*)* Dear lady, we have a lovely person at the church, a counselor, well-trained—

ELEANOR: *Bugger off! (She rushes upstairs and exits.)*

(Beat. Looking after her:)

MR BUTTS: My my my my.

(LOLLY *moves back to the fireplace,* MR BUTTS *remaining at foot of stairs, facing her, his back to french doors.*)

LOLLY: Sad.

MR BUTTS: Tragic.

LOLLY: You should have known her as a girl. So lovely, so shining, so trusting.

(THE GHOST *reappears, through french doors, behind, and unseen by,* MR BUTTS. *Slouching, shirtless as before, bathed in golden morning light. He stares from the garden at* LOLLY)

MR BUTTS: Did she mention the name "Gregory"?

LOLLY: (*Turning from mantle, with a deprecating wave of her hand*) Oh, that was— (*Startled, seeing* THE GHOST, *the words catch.*)

(*Beat*)

MR BUTTS: Is there something wrong, Miss C?

(THE GHOST *stretches sensuously and yawns.*)

LOLLY: (*Recovering herself*) Well, the mundane fundraising world calls out for you, Butts.

MR BUTTS: (*Checking watch*) Indeed it does. But I won't forsake our beautiful dream of the past. The dashing, exciting past—

(*Crossing,* LOLLY *steers* MR BUTTS *out the door*)

LOLLY: But duty calls, I know. There'l be other visits, more research—

MR BUTTS: But nothing will change *us*—about *him*. You know, I can almost *see* him.

LOLLY: (*Pumping his hand*) Now now. Don't get *too* carried away. Ta-ta, good old Butts.

MR BUTTS: Good-bye, dear Miss C. (*He exits.*)

(After closing door on him, LOLLY *turns slowly round to confront the spectre in the garden. To* THE GHOST:)

LOLLY: So. You fell asleep in the garden.

*(*THE GHOST *rubs eyes with knuckles.)*

LOLLY: She *didn't* see you. You don't show yourself to *her* anymore, do you?

*(*THE GHOST *smiles at her and scratches his naked torso.* LOLLY *giggles and covers her lower face with fan.)*

LOLLY: Drowsy brat. And no wonder, after last night.

*(*THE GHOST *starts to move off.)*

LOLLY: *(Lowering fan)* Where are you going? Down to the rocks?

*(*THE GHOST *pauses, hooking his fingers in his trousers, and regards* LOLLY, *expressionless)*

LOLLY: Yes, we *should* get some sun. I'll change and meet you. I'll bring my sketchpad.

*(*THE GHOST *shrugs.)*

LOLLY: Don't do that, Gregory. That bored look you get, I can't stand it. Did you give *her* that look? Your poor wife?

*(*LOLLY *moves into garden, approaching* THE GHOST. *She reaches out to caress his naked chest. He is impassive)*

LOLLY: I'll do anything, Gregory...*I* won't fail you. *(She descends to her knees, lightly kissing his torso)*

(The phone rings, loudly)

*(*THE GHOST *grasps* LOLLY *brutally by the hair, turning het away from audience)*

(The phone rings off the hook.)

(Blackout)

Scene 6

(The same, the following morning. Sunlight from the garden.
LOLLY *is at her easel, center of the room, wearing a pretty*
sundress, bonnet hanging down behind, obsessively painting
a watercolor we cannot see. Teakettle hisses, off.)

LOLLY: *Damn!* The kettle.

(Exits hastily into kitchen. Teakettle ceases as ELEANOR
appears, top of stairs. Hungover, she descends with
difficulty, her hair a mess, robe slovenly and untied, a dirty
wrinkled slip beneath—a fullblown slattern. Shields her eyes
from afternoon sun streaming in from the garden, crosses
into the room, glancing at easel on her way to sideboard.
Double-take. Gasps, shocked at what she sees there. LOLLY
enters from kitchen with a cup of tea.)

ELEANOR: Good god!

LOLLY: Don't make another scene.

ELEANOR: Can't work on this in the *broad sunlight*, can
you?

LOLLY: I should think the scene you made yesterday, in
front of poor old Butts, about meets your quota for the
week.

ELEANOR: And what do you *call* this masterpiece of
pornography?

LOLLY: I call it a beautiful pursuit for a long afternoon.

ELEANOR: *Beautiful?* This old virgin's vision of
paradise?

LOLLY: You seem to have my virginity on the brain.

ELEANOR: Only a woman who's never *once* touched a
man could imagine anything so fantastically graphic!

LOLLY: I paint the truth. The truth is fantastic.

ELEANOR: Don't you think your delusions have gone
far enough?

(LOLLY *brushes past* ELEANOR.)

LOLLY: *(Sips, sips tea, resumes painting)* If you've come down to apologize for yesterday, you're not succeeding.

ELEANOR: *I* apologize? After that jealous snit of yours?

LOLLY: You know damn well you're the jealous one, Eleanor.

ELEANOR: *(Crossing to mantle)* Lolly, you're jealous of my past. Jealous that I *have* a past. So sick with envy that you'd even say that Gregory—of all people!—was *(Laughs)* a poofter!

LOLLY: I never said a word against Gregory. *You're* the one who thinks he's— "that way".

ELEANOR: *What?*

LOLLY: From the first moment you saw him, up there in your room, you've wanted him. And because he prefers *me*—

ELEANOR: Are you talking about that…that idiotic *spectre*? You mean you had the gall to call it *Gregory*?

LOLLY: "It"? You refer to that splendid boy as "it"?

ELEANOR: Don't you see what you're doing? You're filling up your empty, loveless life with details out of *mine*. You're dressing up *your* fantasies—

LOLLY: *Whose* fantasies? You said you saw him only yesterday, entering through the garden.

ELEANOR: Lolly, I was—

LOLLY: Drunk, I know. And I believe you. You *did* imagine him. Because he'll never again show himself to *you*. He despises you.

ELEANOR: Lolly, hallucinations cannot hate *or* love.

LOLLY: You should know. After all, you spent *years* running after a homosexual hustler, and if *that* doesn't rate as hallucination

ELEANOR: Gregory was no spook! He was *real*!

LOLLY: Was he?

ELEANOR: And he *wasn't* a pervert!

LOLLY: Whatever he was, can you say he was real? After duping you for so long? He made promises, didn't he? That he'd stay with you, perhaps even marry you—

ELEANOR: *(Turning away, hands over ears)* I'm *not* like you! You can't make me crazy!

LOLLY: No, you're not like me at all. Because *he's* not like a material man.

ELEANOR: He?

LOLLY: *My* Gregory. He's realer than the material. He's on a higher astral plane, as they call it in Burbank.

ELEANOR: Bugger Burbank! You're mad.

LOLLY: I'm fulfilled. You never have been.

ELEANOR: The source of your insanity, Lolly, is that you've never been *in* your body. You've never been grounded. *(Bitterly)* Bedded.

LOLLY: Really?

ELEANOR: You've never known real pain *or* real pleasure.

LOLLY: *(Dabbing at watercolor)* Haven't I?

(Beat. ELEANOR *watches* LOLLY *paint. She moves— irresistibly drawn—to look over her cousin's shoulder. Shaking her head:)*

ELEANOR: You're lucky he's *not* real. You'd have trouble *walking*!

LOLLY: Oh, that's only a minor part of it.

ELEANOR: Part of *what*?

LOLLY: Of our love-making.

(Beat)

(ELEANOR crosses to mantle, leans against it, regarding LOLLY.)

ELEANOR: All right, Lolly. Out with it. I'm listening.

(LOLLY rises from her easel.)

LOLLY: Tea?

ELEANOR: No, thank you.

LOLLY: I'm off coffee.

ELEANOR: Are you?

LOLLY: Agitating.

ELEANOR: Oh, very.

(LOLLY crosses to a table, from which she takes up the antique lacquered fan. Spreads and contracts it as she wanders about, talking)

LOLLY: I don't say it's anything like making love to a material man. Whatever *that's* like. As you are fond of pointing out, I'm a virgin. Perhaps that's why he chose me instead of you.

ELEANOR: Or perhaps it likes *older* women.

LOLLY: *(Halting) Stop* using the impersonal pronoun, Eleanor.

ELEANOR: Sorry.

LOLLY: "It" won't quite do, and you know it.

(ELEANOR turns away.)

LOLLY: Before you realized he was mine, you were willing enough to admit his existence. But now you want me to think I'm insane, don't you?

ELEANOR: *(Turning back)* It's as I told you yesterday. We're imagining him. Not so very remarkable—two lonely women in a remote place. But do go on.

LOLLY: With my *fantasy*?

ELEANOR: Oh, it has a *pathological* fascination.

LOLLY: *(Resumes wandering about)* I'm sure. Well, it *is* a matter for wonder. For instance, I did wonder at his preference. As to age there's not much to choose between us. But you were always—you still are— the prettier one. Even taking your dissipation into account, the ravages, the puffiness—

ELEANOR: No need, darling, for a laundry list of my imperfections.

LOLLY: Sensitive! Well, I'm not. God knows, I've always been what they call in California a "skag". For years I fought against it, but finally a woman can never rise above her body-type, can she? Men slot you into a category, and there you stay, caught for all time in anatomical amber. So naturally I was surprised when he passed you over and settled on plain old me. Though between a middle-aged frump and an aging alcoholic—

ELEANOR: Yes, it was obviously *slim pickings* for the poor thing, but do get to the point, Lolly.

LOLLY: The point?

ELEANOR: The *dirty* part.

LOLLY: The point, Eleanor, is that he isn't an ordinary man. Not like men living today.

ELEANOR: Oh, we've all had fantasies of a swashbuckling lover out of *Anthony Adverse*.

LOLLY: He's *not* a creation of Hollywood. Neither is he bound by conventions or passing standards. He's free. He's large.

ELEANOR: *(Ironic; glancing pointedly at easel)* Whopping!

LOLLY: Oh, I don't say he isn't lusty. It was part of his life, and it burns in him still. An unappeasable hunger. *(Pausing by easel)* That's what I was trying to catch here. It's not that he's intent on achieving some wretched penile blurt. He's not a *modern* man, with lusts the size of his stunted horizons.

ELEANOR: Good god, that's prose out of a dollar-fifty gothic!

LOLLY: He's a force of nature! Open, unashamed, irresistible. I suppose that's essentially why he chose me.

ELEANOR: I beg your pardon?

LOLLY: He required a kind of purity.

ELEANOR: Sweet of you to say it.

LOLLY: Oh, I don't mean sexual purity. I mean a purity in the nerves. Clear, trusting, unbruised nerves. He *didn't* want to possess a paranoid person.

ELEANOR: So you admit it. You're possessed.

LOLLY: Isn't a woman always? By the simple weight of a man, the smell of him?

ELEANOR: You *smell* him?

LOLLY: Of course. Pretty rank, actually. But then everything about him is intense.

ELEANOR: Yes, men do have characteristic body odors. What's *his* like?

LOLLY: Beans.

ELEANOR: *Beans?*

LOLLY: Baked beans.

ELEANOR: How appropriate, as Boston's so close. So throughout your—congress—he's more or less human? Substantial. Glandular.

LOLLY: Smooth. Juicy. On the mechanical level, yes.

ELEANOR: Well, that's the level I'm interested in.

LOLLY: Yes, I was only interested in the mechanics, too, at first. But aren't we always? Initially we want the physical thrill, don't we? And then that's not enough, and we want something else, we're not sure what. And it's precisely there, I take it, that material men don't deliver.

ELEANOR: Back to the *beany* level. What does he—*do* to you?

LOLLY: You want the details.

ELEANOR: Be as graphic as that painting.

(LOLLY *lowers fan to her side and faces* ELEANOR. *Cold, flat, relentless:*)

LOLLY: He burrows into me, like an animal. He gets *inside* me, Eleanor, I mean *really* inside me. Climbs right into me. As if I were a suit of clothes. He pushes and strains. Pokes his fingers into my fingers, fills my tongue with his—I can even feel his skull inside mine, bone scraping bone—

ELEANOR: (*A mixture of panic and jealousy*) Lolly! He's *devouring* you!

(*Beat, as* LOLLY *regards* ELEANOR *loftily. With a toss of her hair:*)

LOLLY: He's magnificent.

ELEANOR: Aren't you afraid?

LOLLY: Of what? (*Snapping the fan*) Of blending with a force of nature? Of looking at the sea and expanding with *his* dreams? Of seeing the world as an achingly gorgeous animal to be dominated and conquered? Of feeling *brave* for the first time in my life?

(Beat, as ELEANOR *and* LOLLY *stare into each other's eyes.* ELEANOR *is the first to look away)*

ELEANOR: Go on, Lolly.

*(*ELEANOR *crosses to fireplace and gazes into mirror over mantle, beginning, tentatively, to fix her dishevelled hair, as* LOLLY *continues pacing, working the fan)*

LOLLY: Of course, I don't say we haven't had our ups and downs. Sometimes I feel him inside me, other times— *(Halts by french doors, looking out)* —I see him out there, drifting away from me. But every day that passes, sees us a little more mixed, a little more cemented.

(Beat, as ELEANOR *turns from mirror, regarding* LOLLY *closely)*

ELEANOR: *(Sympathetically)* It's beautiful.

LOLLY: *(Turning away from french doors)* Oh, so now it's beautiful. Before, he didn't even *exist*!

ELEANOR: Darling, forgive me. Can't we bury the hatchet? I think I understand now.

LOLLY: Who knows *what* you understand, Eleanor?

ELEANOR: I understand what this…this man means to you. He's the love of your life.

LOLLY: Oh, Eleanor, if only you *could* sympathize—

ELEANOR: How could I not? You're living in a kind of ecstasy, where pain and pleasure are indistinguishable. It's a sight to touch any woman's heart, who's been through it. It's compelling.

LOLLY: What it is, is amazing.

ELEANOR: You're exalted.

LOLLY: Beyond my wildest dreams.

ELEANOR: You've been granted an experience that few women, I daresay, have ever known. I feel privileged.

LOLLY: You?

ELEANOR: To observe it, to be involved in it, in my peripheral way. When a woman's in love, she needs another woman to talk to. How much more a woman in *your* position—

LOLLY: I've *ached* to talk about it. I can't talk to Butts about him anymore—*he* still thinks of Gregory as a romantic *notion*.

ELEANOR: Exactly. *Now* I can be useful, Lolly. *That's* been the trouble. I've felt so *useless*. So shut out. You were so quick to condemn me. But I only wanted to— understand. Now I do.

LOLLY: If *only* you'd stop drinking

ELEANOR: I shall.

LOLLY: No more scenes or ugly words?

ELEANOR: This is an adventure! I'll *back* you!

LOLLY: You'll be my old exquisite Eleanor?

ELEANOR: And you my bossy old Lolly.

LOLLY: (*Tears welling*) I feel so *alone* when he isn't with me!

(ELEANOR *and* LOLLY *embrace,* LOLLY *burying her face in* ELEANOR'*s shoulder*)

ELEANOR: I'll see you through it.

LOLLY: He's so *demanding*!

ELEANOR: He's no different from other men in *that* respect. Tell me something, Lolly. Were you already… *involved* with him when I arrived here?

LOLLY: (*Lifting her face*) Oh no, he was only teasing me then. Touching me, and—well, actually at first he did try to scare me. Heaving his cutlass and all. But I wasn't as frightened as I might have been. You see, he always had his shirt off—

ELEANOR: Yes, yes. But when did you start—*doing* it?

LOLLY: Oh, I'll never forget that night. It was the night after you made all those…insinuations. About his…his tendencies. Of course even then I knew better.

ELEANOR: But he was so open with you! And so *standoffish* with me. Almost as if he meant— *(Beat, as she reflects)* To pit us against each other. From the very start.

LOLLY: Eleanor! He's not *devious*. It's just that he preferred me. I'm sorry about it, of course, but that's the way—

ELEANOR: The cookie crumbles, yes. Well, I did my best, didn't I, with those insinuations? Funny. Laughing at his manhood was the only tactic that got results—with *my* Gregory. No, it's obvious. It's you the ghost wants.—

LOLLY: I was right, wasn't I, Eleanor? About *your* Gregory. He wasn't married, he was a—?

(ELEANOR rises, crosses to easel, looks at watercolor)

ELEANOR: Yes. It was bloody difficult to believe, after running after him for so long, that there could be any— *real* men, dead or alive.

LOLLY: Poor Eleanor. *(Beat)* Damn it! I feel one minute like crying, the next like laughing—

ELEANOR: *(Returning to her cousin)* Lolly, the thing to do is keep busy. Now stop sniffling and go into the kitchen. Make us some lunch.

LOLLY: Yes, you're right.

ELEANOR: Some sandwiches. And I shall go upstairs and get human again. Your pretty dress quite puts me to shame.

LOLLY: You'll *be* here for me?

ELEANOR: To the hilt.

LOLLY: God, I *am* hungry. It's crazy. *(She rises and starts for kitchen.)*

ELEANOR: Lolly?

LOLLY: *(Pausing)* Yes, sweets?

(ELEANOR crosses back to easel and indicates watercolor.)

ELEANOR: May I have this?

LOLLY: I thought you hated it. I grant you, it's not very good.

ELEANOR: But I see it now. The—*astral force* of it.

LOLLY: Fess up. Is it a good likeness?

ELEANOR: How should *I* know?

LOLLY: I meant the *face*, Eleanor. You did see him that once.

ELEANOR: Oh, I knew it was him, didn't I, instantly.

LOLLY: Pretty daring.

ELEANOR: Well, I'm *not* going to hang it over the mantle. I'd simply like to have it.

LOLLY: Sure, if you want it. It's only a study. I haven't captured him yet.

ELEANOR: No.

(As LOLLY exits into kitchen:)

LOLLY: We'll have—*tuna melts*!

(ELEANOR stands looking at watercolor. Peels it from easel. Crosses and ascends stairs, glaring at it. At the top of the

stairs, she pauses. Slowly, viciously, she rips the water-color to shreds and exits)

LOLLY: *(Offstage; from kitchen)* Oh, Eleanor. I forgot. *(Re-entering)* You *hate* fish. How about—? *(She pauses, startled at empty room)*

(The phone rings. LOLLY jumps. It rings again. She reluctantly picks it up.)

LOLLY: Hello?

VOICE: *(Raspy) You like it, don't you?*

LOLLY: What?

VOICE: *You'd die for it, wouldn't you?*

LOLLY: Who is this?

VOICE: *I'm upstairs, Lolly-Pops. Come up and get it!*

LOLLY: Who are you?

VOICE: *Guess!*

LOLLY: You're not Gregory!

(A maniacal cackle. LOLLY drops the receiver, backing away. The cackle escalates to mad, high- pitched laughter that fills the stage. She clasps her hands over her ears)

(Blackout)

Scene 7

(Violent storm. Middle of the night, some days later. The room is dark, illumined only by frequent lightning flashes. Entering from garden, LOLLY bursts, as if driven, into the room, nightdress drenched, her robe torn. She scrambles around the furniture, panicked, as if fleeing an invisible stalker.)

LOLLY: I won't! You can't make me!

(In the sporadic flashes of lightning, we see LOLLY *flung against the fireplace, where she seems to be fending off blows from an invisible hand.)*

LOLLY: Stop it!

*(*LOLLY *breaks away from fireplace, and rushes for stairs. Stumbles over furniture, falls. In a series of bright flashes of light, an opened magazine is seen hovering in mid-air, like an evil bird; it swoops, madly, across the stage straight for her face. She screams and slaps it away.)*

LOLLY: Gregory! For god's sake!

(Furniture inexplicably begins flying about. LOLLY *staggers to her feet and grabs a lamp as it flies past her.)*

LOLLY: You're acting like a child!

(Kitchen door flies open. A butcher knife whizzes out of kitchen and embeds itself in wall a few inches from LOLLY's *head.)*

LOLLY: That's *enough*!

*(*LOLLY *yanks knife from wall and leaps into center of room, defensively jabbing at the air with the blade.)*

LOLLY: I'm from California, buddy boy!

(A crashing sound behind LOLLY. *She spins to face it. Suddenly she drops knife and screams, jumping about as if something is goosing her beneath nightdress. Falls, wriggling, onto floor. She extracts the same magazine as before, now rolled up, from between her legs and flings it away.)*

LOLLY: Think you're *cute*, don't you???

*(*LOLLY's *head begins striking the floor, her hands grappling with invisible fingers at her throat. Strangled cries. Thunder and lightning)*

*(Then—*ELEANOR's *alarmed voice from top of stairs:)*

ELEANOR: *Who's down there?*

(Everything stops. Only the sound of rain. LOLLY collapses, gasping as if released. French doors to garden slam shut. Beat)

ELEANOR: Lolly?

(LOLLY groans.)

ELEANOR: What in the world—

(ELEANOR descends fearfully. Switches on light, illuminating the room. She is seductively clad in her clingiest silken nightgown.)

ELEANOR: *(Looking about)* Good god! What happened here? *(Sees LOLLY)* Lolly! *(Rushes to her, crouches)* My god, Lolly, are you hurt?

LOLLY: Go to bed, Eleanor.

ELEANOR: You're sopping!

LOLLY: It doesn't matter.

ELEANOR: *(Helping LOLLY to her feet)* Pneumonia matters! Get out of those wet things.

LOLLY: Filthy bastard!

ELEANOR: Lolly!

LOLLY: *(Hands to face)* What am I saying?

(ELEANOR helps LOLLY to the settee.)

ELEANOR: Darling, what's wrong? You've been so happy these past few days.

LOLLY: *(Pushing ELEANOR away)* That's right—*gloat*!

ELEANOR: What?

LOLLY: You heard me! Puff up and *gloat*!

ELEANOR: Gloat?

LOLLY: You were right! *(Hands to her face again)* You said he'd want the last drop.

ELEANOR: Take off that sodden robe.

LOLLY: He hates me now.

ELEANOR: Calm down. (*She removes* LOLLY's *wet robe.*) What a pretty little nightgown. Here. Wrap yourself in the comforter.

(ELEANOR *arranges comforter over* LOLLY's *legs.* LOLLY *is dazed through all this, then focusses on* ELEANOR)

LOLLY: Is that—new?

ELEANOR: My nightdress? No, I've had it for years. (*She crosses to french doors, closes drapes.*) Why don't I make some tea? Irish Breakfast? We're out of Oolong.

LOLLY: He's out there, you know.

ELEANOR: Outside? In this storm?

LOLLY: He loves storms. He's down on the beach by now. He watches.

ELEANOR: For what?

LOLLY: For ships, breaking up on the rocks. He hopes for plunder. He *wants* them to break up.

ELEANOR: Quaint of him. I don't suppose many ships do, these days. Comfy?

LOLLY: Get the tea, Eleanor.

ELEANOR: Coming. (*She crosses in direction of kitchen; she stumbles over magazine opened on floor. Bending to pick it up*) My god, what a mess. Bric-a-brac everywhere, magazines—

LOLLY: That's no accident, Eleanor. He left it there. For me. So that I'll see it.

ELEANOR: He reads *magazines*?

LOLLY: And newspapers. He's very well-informed. He leaves it everywhere I go, Eleanor. Opened to exactly that page.

(ELEANOR *looks at magazine, reads:*)

ELEANOR: "The Hashish Connection. The Illegal Brown Haze from Morocco." *(She looks up quizzically at* LOLLY.*)*

LOLLY: He wants me to go there.

ELEANOR: To Morocco?

LOLLY: The Barbary Coast. That's how *he* remembers it.

ELEANOR: But why?

LOLLY: He's—*bound* to this house. To this stretch of coast. Naturally he's restless.

ELEANOR: Bound?

LOLLY: To the place he died. Unfulfilled. Frustrated.

ELEANOR: He's frustrated?

LOLLY: He's *torturing* me!

*(*LOLLY *breaks down again.* ELEANOR *places magazine on table and goes to comfort her)*

ELEANOR: Why didn't you come to me before?

LOLLY: I wasn't sure, We don't—*talk*, you see.

ELEANOR: Lolly, we've been talking up a storm. We're *confidantes*.

LOLLY: I mean *he* doesn't talk to me. I have to pick things up.

ELEANOR: Pick what up?

LOLLY: His yearnings, damn it! His desires. He often communicates—telepathically, or by things, like that magazine. He prefers that I simply *know.* Intuitively.

ELEANOR: He's a man, all right, through and through.

LOLLY: I suppose I've been ignoring this particular message for days. Pushing it out of my mind. I was so happy—! But tonight I knew. That magazine was on the bed. *He* wasn't. I waited for him. I couldn't feel him, see him, smell him. It was death. Finally I was drawn to my window. He was out there, looking up at me. The rain had plastered the hair to his forehead, drenching his shirt. The flesh had soaked through the cloth. His nipples, I could see the hair around his nipples—

ELEANOR: Yes, of course. But what does he *want*?

(LOLLY *suddenly rises to her feet.*)

LOLLY: He wants me to— *(Beat) To smuggle for him!*

ELEANOR: To *what*?

LOLLY: *(Agitated pacing)* To go to Morocco. To cop a kilogram of that damned hash. To smuggle it through customs!

ELEANOR: But whatever *for*?

LOLLY: For *him*! As an extension *of* him.

ELEANOR: He wants *you*—?

LOLLY: Don't you understand? He failed in his last caper. Now he wants to atone for it. He wants to pull one off!

ELEANOR: I can't believe that he'd—

LOLLY: Oh, it's not the first time. That woman who lived here, he also asked *her* to do something like this.

ELEANOR: *Aunt Cumber?*

LOLLY: Of course not. He hardly bothered *haunting* her.

ELEANOR: But wait a moment. Didn't Mister Butts say that Aunt C was down on the rocks when she died? With a police flash?

LOLLY: So?

ELEANOR: Trying to give conflicting signals to *passing ships*?

LOLLY: Eleanor, she was a crazy old woman. Gregory has better taste than to possess *her*. I meant that Sturdevant woman he was married to. When they hung him. He came back to ask her to do something like this, she couldn't bring herself, and the conflict drove her mad. Now I know what she was going through.

ELEANOR: And what about the crank phone calls?

LOLLY: Don't be an idiot. Gregory would never stoop to *that*. It's some local cracker, I'm sure of it. Don't you see? He wants the ultimate—

ELEANOR: But he seriously believes that you—*you!*— would smuggle for him?

LOLLY: Well? Who would suspect *me*? A middle-aged spinster, a school-teacher on holiday. I'd probably *sail* through customs.

ELEANOR: But to ask you, of all people, to commit a *crime*—

LOLLY: Oh, I don't mind *that*.

(Beat)

ELEANOR: You don't—mind?

LOLLY: *That's* not what terrifies me.

ELEANOR: *(Rising)* I'll get the tea.

LOLLY: To hell with the tea! Help me. Tell me I'm right. I've got to refuse him.

ELEANOR: Of course you've got to. It's mad. You, a dope smuggler.

LOLLY: Smuggling? That's a cakewalk. I'd do it in two minutes, if—

ELEANOR: If what?

LOLLY: If I weren't afraid of risking him.

ELEANOR: *You'd* be taking all the risks. It's *you* they'd put in jail.

LOLLY: It *would* be a kind of prison. If I lost him.

ELEANOR: Lost him?

LOLLY: Can't you see?

(Beat)

ELEANOR: *(Idea slowly dawning)* I *do* see. If you go to Morocco, if you bring him this booty, then—*you put his soul to rest*!

LOLLY: *(Sinking at once onto settee)* Exactly. I exorcise him.

(ELEANOR goes to mantle, lights a cigarette from box, turns to face LOLLY)

ELEANOR: We need a drink. *(She crosses to sideboard)*

LOLLY: I'm not as strong as I thought. Am I?

ELEANOR: No. *(Fixing drinks)* But then who would be?

LOLLY: I don't want to lose him, Eleanor!

ELEANOR: *(Extending drink)* Darling, only *you* could have seen the danger.

LOLLY: *(Taking drink, looking about)* Where's my fan?

ELEANOR: *(Drinking; to herself)* What an adventure.

LOLLY: Where can it be?

ELEANOR: Darling, lie back. Get under the comforter.

LOLLY: But I need it! I want it!

ELEANOR: What, the fan? I'll find it for you.

(ELEANOR gets LOLLY to lie back under comforter.)

ELEANOR: There. *(Looking about)* Well, I'm glad you're not being *romantic* about this.

LOLLY: Romantic?

ELEANOR: And darling, I don't in the least think it selfish of you.

LOLLY: Selfish?

ELEANOR: You're finally being realistic.

LOLLY: I am?

ELEANOR: *(Straightening room)* Of course. A romantic would have seen it as a question of *sacrifice*.

LOLLY: What?

ELEANOR: You know. That sometimes you have to risk everything—for your lover. You have to do what's right for *him.* The romantic would have gone to Morocco. She would have smuggled for him. As a sacrifice.

LOLLY: You mean that by putting his soul to rest—?

ELEANOR: *(Picking up overturned table)* Precisely. You sacrifice your petty happiness for his eternal peace. You release him from his bondage to this house. You quiet him. Forever. Idealistic twaddle.

LOLLY: But he doesn't *want* to be quieted!

ELEANOR: *(Crouching to pick up debris)* Well, that hardly signifies, does it? I mean, in the romantic view of it. You do what is spiritually "right," don't you see? Sodding asinine.

(Back to LOLLY, ELEANOR *discovers fan in debris. She snatches it up and rises, spreading it out, looking at it, as:)*

LOLLY: He'd be bored *stiff* by eternal peace!

ELEANOR: *(Back to* LOLLY, *regarding fan)* You're damned right he would.

LOLLY: Only, he doesn't *see* the danger. Doesn't *care* about consequences. He simply wants his— *(Bitterly)* Booty.

ELEANOR: *(Secreting fan in bodice and turning round)* Of course. He's a child. A typical male. *(Crossing slowly to* LOLLY*)* The romantic girl would imagine the highest good to consist in giving him peace. But the realistic girl knows that the *only* good is in keeping him by her side. Ruthless? Some might say so. Hard? Yes, they always apply *that* term. Self-serving? Well, in reality, who isn't? Especially where love is concerned

LOLLY: *(Agitated)* Find my fan, Eleanor. *(Rising up)* I feel amputated without it.

ELEANOR: Oh, how stupid of me. I meant to tell you. It just suddenly *appeared* in my room. As if by magic. Forgot to bring it down to you.

(Beat)

LOLLY: *(Staring at* ELEANOR*)* You have—my fan?

ELEANOR: Perhaps you were in my room and dropped it. Shall I pop up and get it?

LOLLY: *(Lying back again; peering at* ELEANOR*)* No. Don't bother, Eleanor.

ELEANOR: At last you're living in the *real* world. *(Picks up drink, sips)* No, you mus'n't go to Morocco.

LOLLY: *(Growing suspicion)* No?

ELEANOR: But the problem is, how to handle him, now you've refused. I mean, what *can* he do about it?

LOLLY: *(Very, very suspicious)* Well, look around you.

ELEANOR: Oh, of course—his *tantrums.* But he'll soon grow tired of that. He'll crawl back ,to you. You're all he's got.

LOLLY: So you think I'd be—*romantic*? If I were to do as he asks.

ELEANOR: Of course. You're a realist now. Wait him out.

LOLLY: Yes, that would give you all *sorts* of time, wouldn't it?

ELEANOR: Time?

LOLLY: *(Snapping forward)* Time to offer *yourself* for the job!

ELEANOR: Darling, what *are* you—?

LOLLY: Did he give you my fan, Eleanor? Have I forced him to appeal to *you*? I should have *known*. Been trotting out all your prettiest clothes, haven't you? Making yourself receptive. Understanding. Sympathetic. *Sober!* Waiting for him to *try* you again!

ELEANOR: He doesn't want *me*. You know that.

LOLLY: He'll take what he can get! Even you!

ELEANOR: Thank you. And the fan—?

LOLLY: Was an act of despair. He's trying to make me jealous. Trying to make me *see*.

ELEANOR: Bit of a prick, then, isn't he?

LOLLY: His nature is his nature. I see him, now, as clearly as I see you.

ELEANOR: Me?

LOLLY: Yes. Once you've gotten me to refuse, you think you'll be able to draw him to yourself. You'd promise him the moon and Morocco to get him away from me. You'd string him along, manipulate him—just so long as you get what you're after.

ELEANOR: Which is?

LOLLY: *The first honest bang you've had in years!*

(Beat)

ELEANOR: You're not only snapping, you're vicious. But then you're upset.

LOLLY: Has he been with you?

ELEANOR: Well, suppose I have *felt* him a little. What does that portend? And even if I do *see* him now and then—

LOLLY: You've *seen* him? He's started *showing* himself to you again?

ELEANOR: Darling, how could I avoid it? You and I have been so close these last few days. An occasional glimpse, a mere *whiff* of him—

LOLLY: I'm *going* to Morocco!

ELEANOR: And risk sacrificing your happiness?

LOLLY: I'd sacrifice my soul to him!

ELEANOR: Lolly! After all I've just told you. You're a woman, Lolly. Not a—*heroine*!

LOLLY: I see through you, Eleanor. You don't love him. Before I'd see him in *your* bed? I'd risk *exorcising* him!

ELEANOR: What you *risk*! Is losing the only love you've known in your entire dried-up and desolate existence!

(Beat)

LOLLY: *(Lying back)* Where did you learn these sneaking tricks, Eleanor? During your recent career as a *fruit fly*?

(Beat)

ELEANOR: *(Hard)* Finish your drink.

LOLLY: It's plain as dirt what I have to do.

ELEANOR: You silly, self-destructive—

LOLLY: I'll make plane reservations in the morning. Mention nothing to Butts, to anyone. Oh, I see you so vividly now, and that helps me to see my way. I won't force him into your arms. If I lose him, I lose him. When you love someone, someone pure and strong, you give everything you've got. I was put here to *serve* him. I don't expect you'll appreciate that. Now go away. I need some sleep. I'm— *(Turns over, closing eyes)* —wasted.

(Beat)

ELEANOR: As they say In Burbank.

(ELEANOR *watches* LOLLY *fall into an exhausted slumber.
Then* ELEANOR *rises, still staring at* LOLLY. *Suddenly she
twirls girlishly and giggles, just as abruptly clutches in
panic at her chest. With a muffled cry she rips the fan from
her bosom—as if it were red hot—and throws it on floor. She
stares at it, then at the closed drapes. She snatches up fan
and holds it before her, smoking, in her shaking fist.)*

(Thunder. Lights dim.)

(Slowly ELEANOR *approaches drapes. Hesitantly reaches
out. Rips them open; springs back)*

*(*THE GHOST, *drenched, a dirty knout over his gleaming
loins, cutlass in his teeth, hands and face flattened against
the glass, glowers at* ELEANOR*)*

(Lightning flashes etch him in silver)

(Suddenly, LOLLY, *in her sleep, cries out plaintively:)*

LOLLY: Morocco. Morocco.

*(*ELEANOR *opens the french doors.)*

(Blackout)

Scene 8

*(Morning, two weeks later. Bright sunlight from the garden.
Furniture covered with sheets. Floor strewn with dresses—
mostly gay tropical prints. Opened luggage)*

*(*ELEANOR *descends stairs wearing a diaphanous, revealing
dress and clasping the antique lacquered fan. She is
beautiful, her step lively. She opens french doors to let in
the soft air. Moves into sitting room, popping a chocolate
into her mouth from a gutted candybox. Picks out one of
the bright print dresses and holds it against her, swaying
before the mirror over the mantle and playing with the fan.*

Abruptly she pauses, as if she's heard something. Calling up stairs, her voice, low, husky:)

ELEANOR: Hey, sleepyhead. Are you up?

(A sudden knocking at entrance door. Startled, ELEANOR *drops the dress. Beat. Smoothing her gown, she crosses to door, opens it)*

ELEANOR: *(Coldly)* Why, Mister Butts. How unexpected.

(Enter MR BUTTS*)*

MR BUTTS: Condolences, dear lady. I'm speechless.

ELEANOR: *(Showing him into room)* I beg your pardon?

MR BUTTS: I don't at all know what to say. But I thought I'd better come by.

ELEANOR: Oh yes. Poor Lolly.

MR BUTTS: Shocking.

ELEANOR: *(Casting sheet from settee)* Sit down, Mister Butts. Coffee?

MR BUTTS: No, I musn't stay. Are you— *(Looking about, as he sits)* —going somewhere?

ELEANOR: Why, yes. Excuse the chaos.

MR BUTTS: Miss C's still in custody, then? In Casablanca?

ELEANOR: For quite awhile, I'm afraid. They take a dim view over there, and she hasn't a leg to stand on.

MR BUTTS: The town's agog. Nobody can believe that one of the Misses Cumber—

ELEANOR: *(Crossing to mantle, lighting a cigarette from box)* Inexplicable, but there it is. I advised her against going. Seemed like such an odd place for a vacation.

MR BUTTS: She couldn't have needed the money, what with your aunt's annuity and so forth.

ELEANOR: No, I think she simply fell in with some persuasive sorts, and lost her bearings. When you're travelling alone in very odd countries. And she always was— *(Snaps fan; looks pointedly at* MR BUTTS*)* Romantic.

MR BUTTS: But such a sweet lady. That's in fact why I can't understand—

ELEANOR: Well, even the best of us can have a reckless impulse.

MR BUTTS: Oh, surely. The human heart— *(Gesture of hopelessness)* An abyss. No, what I don't understand is how they *knew.* Miss C was so— *(Gropes)*

ELEANOR: So matronly?

MR BUTTS: So very sort of conventional, in her own sweet way. So unlikely to have aroused suspicions. And yet the papers said they "pinched" her right away, without even going through her luggage. Apparently they were "tipped off."

ELEANOR: Oh, these drug wars are unfathomable.

MR BUTTS: Very mysterious.

ELEANOR: Quite.

MR BUTTS: *(Shaking his head)* Two great kilos.

ELEANOR: Impressive.

MR BUTTS: *(Same)* A Moroccan jail.

ELEANOR: Unpleasant.

MR BUTTS: But thank god you're going over.

ELEANOR: I? To Morocco? Not in a million years.

MR BUTTS: You're *not* going to see her?

ELEANOR: What can *I* do? I've put a lawyer on it. Apparently it's a matter of bribes. Could take years.

MR BUTTS: Poor, *poor* Miss C!

ELEANOR: We'll do what we can. No, I'm rather in need of a vacation myself. I'm—upset.

MR BUTTS: Of course you are. Back to London?

ELEANOR: Mexico.

MR BUTTS: For the soothing sun.

ELEANOR: Precisely.

MR BUTTS: Well, do be careful.

ELEANOR: Careful?

MR BUTTS: They've drug wars down there, too, you know. All sorts of violence and—

ELEANOR: I'm a seasoned traveller, Mister Butts.

MR BUTTS: Indeed you are. A world traveller.

ELEANOR: I stick to the well-worn tourist paths.

MR BUTTS: You know the ropes.

ELEANOR: I never stray.

MR BUTTS: Well, do wire me when you intend to return. I can pick you up. Save you a taxi.

ELEANOR: Why, Mister Butts, that's very kind. I certainly shall.

MR BUTTS: It's funny, you know. Miss C and I had been discussing—you remember, our little conceit about a ghost?

ELEANOR: Amusing. Fanciful. Lolly liked that sort of thing.

MR BUTTS: Yes. But I hope our harmless little talks didn't—somehow—push her—over the edge

ELEANOR: Yes, romanticism *is* dangerous, isn't it? As you say, a certain type of person can easily lose her balance. But I wouldn't *berate* myself, Mister Butts.

(Beat)

MR BUTTS: Thank you—dear lady.

ELEANOR: Well, I've things to do upstairs.

MR BUTTS: *(Rising)* Yes, I'm off. Soak up the good rays. Return to us tanned and—I hope—less upset.

ELEANOR: *(Showing him to door)* Or perhaps renewed. And don't worry about Lolly. Things will turn out.

MR BUTTS: I've my fingers crossed.

ELEANOR: And I *shall* wire you.

MR BUTTS: Happy to be of assistance.

ELEANOR: Good-bye, Mister Butts.

MR BUTTS: Good-bye, Miss Cumber. *(Starts to leave, turns back)* You know, I've always wanted us to be friends. It gets so lonely here, and conversation is so limited. A woman of your brilliant gifts, you shouldn't hoard them—

ELEANOR: Oh, I don't claim to be as sociable as Lolly. But you're more than welcome— *(With a pronounced shrug)* Anytime.

MR BUTTS: *(Dampened) Bon voyage*, Miss Cumber.

ELEANOR: *A bientôt*, Mister Butts.

(Exit MR BUTTS.*)*

*(*ELEANOR *closes drapes over french doors and moves back into room. Pops a chocolate into her mouth, crosses and picks up a bright print dress. Holds it against her, looking into mirror over mantle. Twirls, snaps fan, and poses)*

(Enter THE GHOST, *top of stairs. He grips banister, his head tilted grotesquely to one side, his expression stern, unsmiling, as he glares down at* ELEANOR. *She sees him in mirror, and addresses her words into it)*

ELEANOR: *(Referring to dress)* Like it?

(Beat, as THE GHOST *continues glowering down at her. Suddenly, dropping dress,* ELEANOR *breaks into a peal of laughter. Abruptly ceasing, into mirror:)*

ELEANOR: Oh, Anthony. Disapproval? From *you*? *(She lights another cigarette from box on mantle, continuing into mirror:)* I know. I should have told you about poor Lolly. But I *had* to inform the authorities, *you* know that.

*(*THE GHOST *shakes his head in disgust)*

ELEANOR: Oh, don't worry, darling. I did it anonymously.

*(*THE GHOST *turns angrily away. Still speaking to mirror, she stops him with:)*

ELEANOR: And Tony. We're talking *heroin* now… It's quite the drug of choice. Much more valuable than hashish. And far more dangerous to import.

*(*THE GHOST *turns slowly back)*

ELEANOR: Yes, I thought you'd like that. So you see, you're better off. Dear, romantic Lolly, she was afraid one might *exorcise* you. Fat chance. *(Picks up poker from stand by fireplace. Rubs it up and down. Arch, into mirror:)* Want to come down, Tony? And play with the poker?

*(*THE GHOST *yawns and scratches his ass.)*

ELEANOR: *(Replacing poker)* Oh no, you'll *never* stop wanting. *(Primping, into mirror:)* I'll go to Mexico. I'll get your—*booty*. And you'll want more. And I'll get it. You'll want something else. I'll get that too. Lolly didn't in the least understand you. *(She raises fan to her chin, snaps it open, and, into mirror, mock-flutters her eyelashes over it. Then she flings it into the fireplace. Turns abruptly to face him. Hard:)* But I do. You *wanted* me to get rid of her, all along. (Crosses and ascends stairs during following:) Another pelt for your collection of destroyed females. Better than mere hashish. That's why you teased me and went after *her*. It wasn't because I belittled your manhood. You *knew* I'd be jealous and add Lolly to your list. Your wife, Aunt Cumber—how many others?

(THE GHOST *smiles, his back to* ELEANOR *as she ascends.*)

ELEANOR: So you see how thoroughly I understand you. Which is why I will *not* be on your list, Tony. (*Arriving top of stairs, she embraces him passionately from behind.*) Oh no. I'm all you've got now. No one but me to commit your crimes. And I don't care. Because every stinking inch of you, Tony—is all man. (*Sensuously, clawing as she withdraws, she releases him. Playfully she tickles his ear. Huskily, sexily:*) Tony?

(THE GHOST *turns round to look at* ELEANOR.)

(*Backing away, unbuttoning her dress,* ELEANOR *seductively exits, smiling back at* THE GHOST.)

(*Beat, as* THE GHOST *licks his lips. He begins to follow her, tearing open his shirt to reveal his naked torso.*)

(*A noise from the garden.* THE GHOST *pauses*)

A MAN'S VOICE: (*Loud whisper*) Smitty?

(*Enter* MR BUTTS, *sneakily, through the french doors, parting the drapes*)

(THE GHOST *gazes down* MR BUTTS, *impassively*)

MR BUTTS: You were supposed to meet me. Down on the rocks.

(THE GHOST *scratches his armpit.*)

MR BUTTS: One down, one to go. I *knew* she'd rat on old Lolly-pops. But don't worry. Eleanor isn't coming back either. *I'll* see ·to that. (*Sniggers*) One in a Moroccan jail, one in a Mexican! They can send each other *postcards*!

(THE GHOST *shakes his head in disdain.*)

MR BUTTS: Then the house reverts to the Church. We can be together!

(With a gesture of disgust, THE GHOST *turns to exit)*

MR BUTTS: Smitty, wait!

*(*THE GHOST *pauses, arms akimbo, waiting.)*

*(*MR BUTTS *drops to his knees and crawls up the stairs, as:)*

MR BUTTS: I did it all for you. All those phone calls. I fed them stories. I drove them crazy. I set it all up, Smitty. For you.

*(*THE GHOST, *with the disdainful toe of his boot, pushes* MR BUTTS *back down stairs.)*

MR BUTTS: But, Smitty, I get my vacation soon. I'm going to *England.* Jeepers, I'll have access to *so* many churches. So many wonderful old churches. I can steal things for you, Smitty. *(He has crawled back up; at* THE GHOST'*s feet, looking up at him worshipfully:) Sacred things!*

(Beat, as THE GHOST *considers this. Suddenly, from offstage:)*

ELEANOR: *(Calling)* Tony? I'm waiting.

*(*MR BUTTS *grasps* THE GHOST'*s boot.)*

MR BUTTS: *(Hissing it)* Come with me! Down to the rocks!

*(*THE GHOST *looks down at* MR BUTTS, *then at the audience.)*

ELEANOR: *(Off; seductively)* Toooonnnny!

MR BUTTS: Altarpieces, Smitty!

ELEANOR: *(Same)* Mexico, Tony.

MR BUTTS: *(Same)* Holy relics!

ELEANOR: *(Same)* Heroin, Tony.

MR BUTTS: *(Same)* Blasphemy!

ELEANOR: *(Same)* Crimes, my darling. Crimes.

(THE GHOST *throws back his twisted head, and his raucous laughter fills the stage as:)*

(The curtain falls.)

END OF PLAY